LITTLE **TOPIC BOOK** OF

Bears

Published 2010 by A&C Black Publishers Limited
36 Soho Square, London W1D 3QY
www.acblack.com

ISBN 978-1-4081-232-25

Text © Judith Harries
Design © Lynda Murray
Photographs © Fotolia

Thank you to Mel Astil for 'Baby Bear is Best' (pages 64-65) and
'Action Bears' (page 73)

A CIP record for this publication is available from the British
Library.

Printed in Great Britain by Latimer Trend & Company Ltd

This book is produced using paper that is made from wood
grown in
managed, sustainable forests. It is natural, renewable and
recyclable.
The logging and manufacturing processes conform to the
environmental
regulations of the country of origin.

To see our full range of titles
visit www.acblack.com

Contents

Introduction

Planning ideas

Well-planned activities in a stimulating learning environment are the key to making children's learning relevant, exciting and effective. Planning should involve all practitioners in the setting working together, sharing ideas and using their combined knowledge of the children to provide appropriate learning experiences.

The Early Years Foundation Stage includes six Early Learning Goals that cover all aspects of the curriculum. All settings need to plan their learning environments carefully to include opportunities for children to develop in each area.

Many early years settings choose to plan around a 'topic' or theme so that the activities are integrated and cross-curricular. This creates connections in children's thinking as they play and results in more meaningful learning. This series of topic books provides a comprehensive collection of ideas and activities for practitioners to 'dip and pick' from when planning.

Looking and listening

Ongoing assessment of children is an essential part of early years planning. Looking, listening and noting down daily observations will help inform future planning so it is appropriate to children's needs and absorbing and relevant to children's interests.

How to use this book

The book is divided up into sections on each of the six Early Learning Goals plus other areas, such as cooking and messy play. Each section contains a set of exciting activities to dip into and select from. Each activity includes links to the relevant Early Learning Goal. The Goals are numbered in the order in which they appear in the Practice Guidance for the EYFS, so, for example, PSED 1 is 'Continue to be interested, excited and motivated to learn'.

Me and my bear

ELG: PSED 1, 2, 3, 7, 8

What you need

- note home to parents inviting children to bring in a special bear from home
- labels
- string
- some spare bears.

What you do

- Invite children to bring in a special teddy bear from home. Make labels for the bears in the style of Paddington Bear (see CLL, Labelling bears, page 11). If a child forgets to bring in a bear of their own, have a supply available for them to 'adopt' for the day.

- Sit in a circle and encourage the children to introduce their bears to the group. Can they tell the children what their bear's name is and talk about his colour, size, history and any distinguishing features?

- In small groups make up stories of adventures that each bear has had with or without their owner! Act them out for the rest of the group.

And another idea

Take photos of each child with their special bear and make into a book or wall display.

Take-away bear

ELG: PSED 2, 4, 5, 8

What you need
- medium-sized teddy bear
- plastic envelope
- paper
- special pencils
- disposable camera.

What you do

- Introduce the 'take-away' bear to the children and decide on a special name for him. Explain that he will go home with a different child each night or weekend to spend time with them and their family. (See sample letter to parent/carer below.)

- Ask each child to record the visit either with a photograph (using the disposable camera), or a picture and some writing.

- Compile this information into a group book.

- Invite the child to speak to the group about their time with 'take-away' bear.

And another idea

Take the bear home yourself and take some photos of him in your home or garden. The children will enjoy seeing that you share in the same activities as them.

Dear parent/carer

(Insert child's name) has been chosen to bring home our special Take-away bear (insert name) today. Please let him join in with all your normal family activities such as going shopping, playing in the garden, eating tea and sharing any bedtime routines. Encourage your child to draw a picture and write a simple sentence of what they do together. It would be great if you could take a photograph too. Please remember to return the bear to school tomorrow.

Thanks for your help and hope you all have fun together.

Moody bear

ELG: PSED 3, 4, 5, 8

What you need
- Mr moody bear jigsaw (available from www.amazon.co.uk)
- teddy bear
- photocopiable bear's head template (see page 77).

What you do

- Use different illustrations of moods on the jigsaw bear to encourage children to identify their own feelings and the feelings of others.

- Make your own moody bear model by drawing different moody expressions on some bear's faces, using the template on page 77. Cut these out and laminate them. Let children use the moody bear pictures to illustrate their feelings.

- Now demonstrate different moods using a teddy bear. Try covering bear's eyes with paws to look scared or sad. Try making the bear jump up and down to show happiness or excitement.

- Talk about why the bear might be feeling sad or happy. Relate to the children's moods. What makes them feel proud, lonely, worried, angry, tired or excited?

- Pass the bear around the circle and encourage less confident children to share their thoughts and feelings. Emphasise that the children can only speak when holding the bear and if they don't want to speak they can pass the bear on.

And another idea
Take some photos or videos of teddy bears showing different moods, for instance covering their face, jumping, lying down, sitting alone and so on. Ask the children to make up stories about why the bear is feeling like that.

Dressing-up bears

ELG: PSED 5,11

What you need

- different-sized teddy bears
- selection of dolls' clothes with different fastenings to fit the bears.

What you do

- Demonstrate how to operate different fastenings such as zips, buttons, Velcro, hook and eye and so on.

- Let the children attempt to dress the teddy bears in appropriate clothes for seasonal weather and manage the different sorts of fastenings. Relate this to the children's own clothes.

- Organise a race and see who can get themselves and their teddy dressed quickest to go out to play.

And another idea

Put up a chart on the wall showing who is able to put on their coat and fasten it ready to go outside or who can get their PE kit on independently.

Teddy bear's picnic

ELG: PSED 4, 5, 8, 12

What you need
- note home to parents inviting children to bring in a special bear from home
- food and drink
- tablecloths
- CD of 'Teddy Bear's Picnic' song.

What you do

- Ask the children to bring in a special teddy bear from home. Invite these bears to come to a teddy bear's picnic. Put up posters and design invitations for the children and carers (see CLL, Picnic invitation, page 16).

- Make honey or marmalade sandwiches, porridge, teddy bear biscuits and oaty flapjacks (see Cooking, Gingerbread bears, page 53, Porridge flapjack, page 54). Serve teddy bear crisps, and jelly with fruit or gummy bears trapped in it. Make chocolate milk to drink. Check for dietary allergies.

- Sit in small groups around the tablecloths and share the food and drink.

- Sing along to the song on the CD and play party games such as 'Musical bumping bears' and 'Musical bear statues'.

And another idea
Try some teddy bear races and sports activities (see Outdoor activities, Ready teddy go, page 43).

'Care bear' puppet

ELG: PSED 3, 4, 9, 10, 13, 14

What you need

- teddy bear puppet (or old teddy bear, needle and thread)
- 'passport' and 'birth certificate' for teddy.

What you do

- Buy a teddy bear glove puppet or make your own. To do this, remove some stuffing from the body of an old bear so that you can insert a hand and operate it like a glove puppet. Over sew the openings so that the remaining stuffing doesn't leak out!

- Introduce the puppet to the children. Devise a history or family background for the bear puppet including a birth certificate and passport. Make the puppet talk in your ear and then tell the children what he said. Only operate this puppet yourself and don't let the children handle it.

- Use the bear as an 'empathy doll' to encourage the children to care for each other. Make up stories about situations that the bear has experienced so that the children can consider 'consequences' and 'right and wrong' such as getting lost, falling out with a friend and stealing.

- Invite the bear to talk to the children about important events he has experienced such as celebrations or festivals.

And another idea

Make a family of bear puppets using different-sized bears or different character bears and act out some of these situations.

Labelling bears
ELG: CLL 3, 10, 11, 15, 18, 19

What you need

- **A Bear called Paddington** or other Paddington Bear stories by Michael Bond (HarperCollins)
- children's own bears
- pre-cut labels
- pens
- string.

Please look after this bear

What you do

Introduce children to the story of Paddington Bear and his origins at Paddington railway station in London wearing a label with the instruction 'Please look after this bear'.

Explain that the children need to design labels for their own bears so that they don't get lost while visiting your setting, especially if it's a special occasion such as the teddy bear's picnic (see PSED, Teddy bear's picnic, page 9).

Show them the pre-cut labels and suggest that they write their bear's name on one side. If their bear doesn't yet have a name try singing the 'Naming song' (see Stories, songs and rhymes page 71).

Help the children to work out how to write the name of their bear by naming and sounding letters from the alphabet.

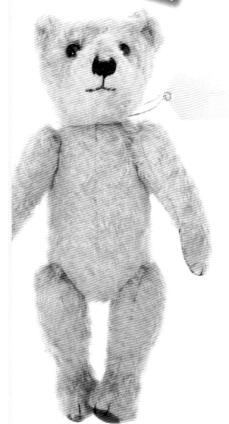

And another idea

Encourage children to write their own names on the reverse of the label by referring to laminated name cards.

Phonic bear

ELG: CLL 2, 5, 9, 10, 11

What you need

- a collection of teddy bears or pictures of bears
- initial letter or phonic cards
- paints
- crayons
- paper.

What you do

- Explore lots of describing words beginning with the letter 'b' to illustrate different bears, for instance Big Bear, Bald Bear, Brave Bear, Bubble Bear, Bashful Bear and so on.

- Invent some alliterative sentences such as 'brave brown bears bounce on my big bed'.

- Repeat with the letter 't' and create Tired Teddy, Timid Ted, Tiny Ted, Terrible Teddy and so on.

- Ask the children to paint or draw pictures of the different bears and make up stories that explain their names!

And another idea

Play around with rhymes and create some rhyming bears such as Care Bear, Share Bear, Fair Bear, Rare Bear, Hair Bear and Stare Bear!

Library of bears

ELG: CLL 2, 3, 4, 13, 15

What you do

- Make a collection of books about bears and set them up as a library so that the children can borrow the books and take them home to share with their families.

- Explain how a library works. Help children to be involved in recording which book they have chosen in a library log and ask them to return it each week.

- Invite the children to read and share these books in the library area and compare stories and illustrations. Include some CD recordings of stories about bears for the children to listen to.

What you need

- varied selection of story and information books about bears (see Useful books, page 75)
- shelves
- comfy chairs and cushions.

And another idea

Organise a trip to the nearest public library and look for more bear stories there. Invite the local librarian to talk to the children about the library service.

'Care bear' storybooks

ELG: CLL 4, 7, 8, 13, 16, 17

What you need
- the 'care bear' puppet (see PSED, 'Care bear' puppet, page 10)
- camera
- paper
- card
- pencils
- crayons

What you do

- Talk about all the different bear stories that the children have enjoyed in the bear library (see Library of bears, page 13).

- Use real or imaginary events to make up stories about your setting's 'care bear' puppet (see PSED, 'Care bear' puppet, page 10).

- Use a camera to take pictures of the bear in different scenarios or ask the children to draw their own illustrations.

- Compile into a group book and put this into the library for the children to read and share.

And another idea
Make tape-recordings of groups of children telling stories about your 'care bear' and put copies in the library for children to listen back to with a friend.

Bear characters

ELG: CLL 2, 3, 4, 6, 8

What you need

- selection of books about famous bears (see Useful books, page 75)
- illustrations of famous bear characters.

What you do

- Talk about famous bear characters from books and films such as Winnie the Pooh, Paddington, Rupert the bear, Old Bear, Threadbear, Big Bear and Little Bear.

- Use storybooks and illustrations to look at the different characteristics that have made each bear famous.

- Help the children to think of questions that they would like to ask each bear.

- Go into role and answer some of the children's questions.

And another idea

Invite the children to choose a favourite famous bear and give the group a reason for their choice. Which is the most popular bear or story among your children (see PSRN, Favourite bears, page 17)?

Picnic invitation

ELG: CLL 1, 11, 17, 18, 19

What you need
- lots of different coloured card
- pens
- printing stamps and inkpads
- stamp addressed envelopes.

What you do

● Talk about the teddy bear's picnic
(see PSED, Teddy bear's picnic, page 9) and the different writing
opportunities it provides. Explain to the children that they are going to
write and send invitations to their bears and/or families.

● Give the children a simple template (see below) to write their invitation
on and then decorate with patterns using pens and stamps.

● Help them to write their name using name cards.

● Can they address the envelopes to their bear or family and then walk to
the nearest post box with an adult to post their letter?

And another idea
Talk about the menu of food for the picnic.
Look at recipes for the biscuits and flapjacks
(see Gingerbread bears, page 53, Porridge
flapjack page 54). Write shopping lists for all
the different ingredients for the picnic food.

Dear _____

Please come to our teddy bears' picnic at

_____

Date _____

Time _____

Don't forget to bring a teddy bear!

Love from _____

Favourite bears

ELG: PSRN 1, 2, 4, 6

What you need
- small pictures of famous bears
- large piece of cardboard
- pens
- glue.

What you do

- Talk to the children about different storybooks about bears and look at the illustrations.

- Show the children lots of small pictures of the bears and ask them to choose their favourite. Make a tally chart to show how many children like each bear.

- Stick the pictures on to a bar chart and ask children to answer some simple questions. Try 'How many children like Winnie the Pooh?', 'Which bear was liked best by four children?' and 'Which bear is the most popular?' (See CLL, Bear characters, page 15).

And another idea
Find another way to display the results such as a pie chart, shaped like a bear's head of course.

My favourite bear is...

Half a bear

ELG: PSRN 4, 9, 10, 11, 12

What you need

- paper, pencils
- bear template (see page 79)
- photocopier,
- coloured pens
- scissors.

What you do

- Talk about symmetry. Ask one child to stand up and place a metre rule down their centre to demonstrate the symmetry of the human body.

- Fold a piece of paper in half and draw the shape of half a bear on one side. Use the bear template as a guide (see page 79).

- Open the sheet out and make a photocopy of it for each child. Ask the children to attempt to draw the other half of the bear exactly the same on the other side.

- Can they decorate their bear picture with a symmetrical pattern using coloured felt-tipped pens?

- Ask the children to cut out the patterned bears.

- Arrange the bears into a colourful display.

And another idea

Try only giving the children a quarter of a bear to complete and decorate.

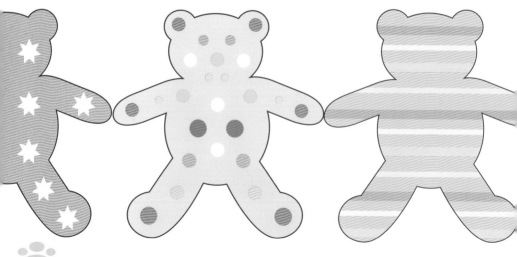

Feed the bears

ELG: PSRN 1, 2, 7

What you need
- soft toy pandas
- green sugar paper
- pens
- scissors.

What you do

- Talk about pandas. Explain that they will only eat bamboo leaves and shoots.

- Draw lots of leaf shapes on green sugar paper and cut them out.

- Ask the children to work with a partner and 'feed' their panda an agreed number of leaves.

- Challenge them with some mathematical questions; 'How many will panda eat if he has one more?' 'If you started with ten, and panda eats three, how many are left?'

- Can the children make up their own game or questions to ask their partner?

And another idea
Try again with brown bears (teddy bears) and fish, cut out of orange sugar paper.

Measuring bears

ELG: PSRN 1, 4, 9, 11

What you need
- collection of different-sized bears
- children's own bears from home
- rulers
- tape measures
- weighing scales.

What you do

- Ask the children to sort the bears into order of size from little to big. Which is the biggest bear?

- Now ask them to use rulers and tape measures to measure the height, width (round the middle!) and head circumference of their own bears.

- Use weighing scales to measure which bear is the heaviest.

- Use the different measurements to order the bears according to height and then weight. Is the heaviest bear also the tallest?

And another idea
Record the information on a record card for each bear with name, weight, height and any other measurements! (See KUW, Bear passports, page 23).

Bear beetle drive

ELG: PSRN 1, 2, 3, 5, 12

What you need

- dice or spinner
- cardboard in four colours
- photocopiable bear parts template (see page 78)
- pens
- scissors.

What you do

- Use the bear spare parts template (see page 78) to create a set of four bears, each from different coloured card. Cut up into separate head, body, two ears, two arms, and two legs.

- Write the numbers 1 to 6 on to the shapes. Draw two eyes on the bear's head (part 1) and a nose and mouth on part 6.

- Let a group of four children play a beetle style game. They should roll the dice or use the spinner, say what the number is then select a bear piece with the corresponding number. See who will be the first to complete their bear picture. (Note: they will need part 1 before adding part 6!)

And another idea

Make a simple lotto game using four different-coloured plastic bears. Draw four windy routes coming from each corner of the page, each divided into 20 steps and ending up in a central circle or Bear cave. Take turns to throw the dice and see which bear gets home first.

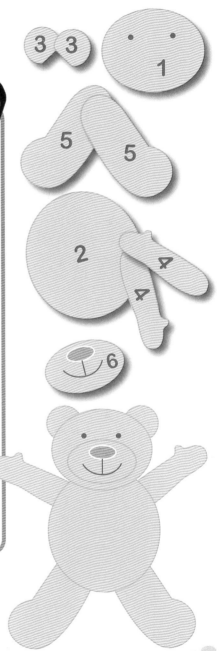

Shape bear

ELG: PSRN 2, 4, 11, 12

What you need

- a range of coloured tissue or sticky paper shapes in different sizes
- glue
- sugar paper.

What you do

- Use some different-sized circles to create the shape of a bear. When the shape is ready stick the circles down, slightly overlapping, on to the sugar paper backing.

- Can the children work out how many of each size circle they used and give instructions to a partner to make a matching 'circle bear'?

- Try again with different shapes. Which shapes work best for the body, or arms and legs? Where could they use a triangle?

- Can they make a bear using two triangles, one circle, one square, and four rectangles?

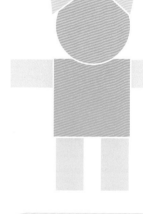

And another idea

Use a 'tap-a-shape' set to create a picture of a bear using hammer, nails and lots of different coloured shapes.

Bear passports

ELG: KUW 2, 4, 7, 8, 9

What you need

- real passports
- special bear from home for each child
- camera
- paper
- stapler
- pens
- pencils.

What you do

- Look at real passports and talk about the information they include, such as photo/picture, birthday and distinguishing features!

- Explain that children can make a passport for their special bear (see PSED, Me and my bear, page 5). Make a booklet of blank pages using paper and a stapler.

- Take a photo of each bear or ask children to draw a mini passport sized picture. Write in the bear's name and measurements (see PSRN, Measuring bears, page 20) and any distinguishing features such as a torn ear, missing eye or bald tummy.

- Add stamps of places the children have taken their bear to on holiday or for outings.

And another idea

Design a front cover for the passport. Look at the emblem on the front of the UK passport with the lion and the unicorn. Can the children design one using a bear?

The story of the teddy bear

ELG: KUW 2, 8, 11

What you need
- an old-fashioned teddy bear
- picture of original cartoon
  (see ICT resources page 74,
  www.theodoreroosevelt.org)
- paper and pencils.

What you do

- Introduce the history of the teddy bear through the story of the US President, Theodore Roosevelt. He went on a bear hunt and after three long days finally came across a very old, tired brown bear. It was too weak to hunt for sport, already injured and in pain, so the President took pity on it and gave orders for it to be put out of its misery.

- Show children the cartoon that a clever political cartoonist drew at the time satirising the event and showing the President refusing to shoot a large bear. A shopkeeper who saw the cartoon took two stuffed toy bears made by his wife and christened them 'Teddy's bears' and they became a popular toy worldwide.

And another idea
Invite the children to draw simple cartoons or pictures of a variety of teddy bears and make a display of them alongside photographs.

Bears around the world

What you need
- information books
- Internet (see ICT Resources, page 74)
- globe or map of the world
- CD-ROMS
- paper
- pencils
- pens.

What you do

- Explain to the children that they are going to research information and produce fact sheets on different bears from around the world.

- Introduce the eight different types of bear - Asian black bear, American black bear, Brown bear (Grizzly), Polar bear, Spectacled bear, Sun bear, Sloth bear and Panda.

- Show the children some of the different areas where these bears can be found, using a globe or map of the world:

    - Asian black bear - India

    - American black bear - North America

    - Brown bear (Grizzly) - Canada

    - Polar bear - Arctic

    - Spectacled bear - South America

    - Sun bear - S.E. Asia

    - Sloth bear - Nepal

    - Panda - China.

- Help them to use the information books, Internet and CD-ROMS to find out about habitat, diet and special characteristics of the bears. Use this information to make simple fact sheets including drawings and photos of the different bears. Scribe simple sentences for the children.

And another idea
Combine the children's research and fact sheets into a book about bears for the library (see CLL, Library of bears, page 13).

Old bears

ELG: KUW 1, 2, 3, 7, 8

What you need

- *Old Bear* by Jane Hissey (Red Fox)
- old and new teddy bears.

What you do

- Read the story of *Old Bear*. This is the story of an old toy bear who has apparently been forgotten and abandoned in the attic only to be rescued by some of his fellow toys.

- Bring in some old teddy bears and invite the children to borrow old bears from their parents and grandparents.

- Make a display of old and new bears and talk about the similarities and differences between them. Look at the different materials used. Do the new bears have moving joints? Have the shapes of the bear's faces changed?

And another idea

Use a camera and ICT such as PowerPoint or Photoshop to create a photo story about the further adventures of an *Old Bear*. Take photos of an old bear finding some new friends and annotate with simple sentences.

Keeping teddy dry

ELG: KUW 1, 2, 3, 4, 6

What you need

- teddy
- a selection of materials, such as cotton wool, felt, plastic, aluminium foil, lace and cardboard
- plastic pots (such as yoghurt pots)
- elastic bands
- child's watering can.

What you do

- Explain to the children that they are going to find out which material is best to make teddy a coat or hat to keep him dry from the rain.

- Can they think of how to create a fair test to investigate which material will be most effective? Allow children the opportunity to experiment with different materials and ideas.

- Encourage the children to predict the results before starting the experiment.

- Choose a variety of materials (see above) and cut out same size circles of each. Place over the top of some empty plastic pots and fasten with elastic band.

- Water each pot with a watering can containing 10ml of water to simulate rain. Remove the fabric and measure how much water has soaked through.

- The material that has let the least water through into the pot should be the most waterproof.

And another idea

Make teddy a hat out of the 'winning' material. Could they try another investigation to discover which material would keep teddy warm?

Dancing bear puppets

ELG: KUW 4, 5, 6, 8

What you need

- old-fashioned string puppets
- cardboard
- photocopiable bear parts template (see page 78)
- photocopier
- scissors
- split pins
- hole punch
- stapler
- string
- thin sticks or dowelling
- sticky tape.

What you do

● Demonstrate some old-fashioned string puppets. Let the children have a go at operating them. Explain that you are all going to make some bear string puppets.

● Help each child to cut out a bear head, body, two arms and two legs from cardboard using the template on page 78. Show the children how to use a hole punch to create five holes in the body and one in each of the other parts.

● Help the children to add the bear's features and then join the parts together loosely using split pins. Take care that all the joints are loose enough for them to move when the puppet dances.

● Cut two lengths of string and staple to the paw end of each arm. Fasten on to the stick and use to operate the puppet.

And another idea

Put on a show using the dancing bear puppets. Who can make their puppet dance the best?

Bear glove puppets
ELG: PD 7, 8

What you need
- a selection of glove puppets
- photocopiable bear's head template (see page 77)
- felt
- old woollen mittens or socks
- sewing needles and thread
- felt-tipped pen
- scissors
- buttons.

What you do

- Let the children explore and try out a selection of different glove or hand puppets. Encourage them to look carefully at how they are constructed.

- Explain that you are going to make some bear glove puppets. Help each child to draw round the head template and cut it out of felt. They can then draw on a face or help them to sew on buttons for eyes.

- Help the children to attach the head to a mitten or sock with a needle and thread.

- Show them how to insert a hand into the mitten or sock to operate their bear puppet.

And another idea
Construct a puppet theatre from a large cardboard box with a window cut from the bottom. Place the theatre box on a table and invite the children to kneel behind and put on a puppet show using their bear puppets.

Bearobics

ELG: PD 1, 2, 4, 5, 6

> ## What you need
> - 'The Bare Necessities' from Disney's Jungle Book sung by Baloo the Bear
> - other dance music
> - balls or small equipment such as beanbags.

What you do

- Talk about keeping healthy by taking exercise such as aerobics and moving to music.

- Introduce 'bearobics' – exercising like bears! Try simple repeated movements such as stepping forward, backward, left, right, punching the air, bending the knees and so on.

- Listen to 'The Bare Necessities' song and try doing the movements in time to the beat of the music.

- Introduce moving with small apparatus such as balls or beanbags.

- Talk to the children about how they feel after exercise. Can they recognise changes in their bodies such as feeling hot? Is their heart beating faster?

And another idea

Watch a clip of 'The Bare Necessities' song on YouTube (www.youtube.com) and copy Baloo and Mowgli's dance steps!

Dancing with bears

ELG: PD 1, 2, 4, 6

What you need

- a selection of music suitable for dancing like bears
- tambourines
- lots of space.

What you do

- Talk about how the children think bears might dance. Look at the painting of Dancing Bears by William Holbrook Beard (see CD, Dancing bears, page 36).

- Demonstrate with lots of stamping, stepping side to side, swaying and hugging!

- Listen to some classical 'bear' music such as Haydn's 'Bear' Symphony, Elgar's Wand of Youth Suite No.2 (The Tame Bear and The Wild Bears) and Bear Dance from Bartok's Hungarian Sketches for Orchestra.

- Let children improvise some dance ideas and then suggest some easy steps for them to follow. Add tambourines and enjoy!

And another idea

For a different style of music and dancing listen and dance along to 'Let me be your teddy bear' by Elvis Presley!

Huggy bears

ELG: PD 1, 2, 4

What you need
- lots of space!

What you do

- Ask the children to move around the room, carefully weaving among each other without bumping or colliding.

- On the shout 'Huggy bears' children must find a friend nearby and have a 'bear hug'.

- Change the shout to 'Huggy threes' or 'Huggy fours' and they have to get into groups of three or four and have a group hug.

And another idea
Let each child play the game carrying their own teddy bear as well. Can the teddy bears have hugs too?

The bear walked over the mountain

ELG: PD 1, 2, 4

What you need
- song 'The Bear Went Over the Mountain'
- drum
- lots of space.

What you do

- Learn the song 'The Bear Went Over the Mountain' and experiment with moving in different ways around the hall. Ask the children to walk around the room as you all sing 'The bear walked over the mountain'.

- Try changing the words and the actions to 'The bear marched…'. Then try these ideas: ran, jumped, climbed, hopped, crept, plodded, bumbled, skied and slid.

- Match the drum beat to the different types of movement: steady beat for walking then faster for running; slow for jumping and climbing; very slow and quiet for creeping; loud and slow for plodding; scraping for skiing and sliding.

And another idea

Use other action rhymes to extend children's skills in moving with control and coordination (see Stories, songs and rhymes, Bears on parade, page 72, Balancing bears, page 73).

Bears' chairs

ELG: PD 2, 7, 8

What you need

- story of *Goldilocks and the Three Bears*
- garden wire
- newspapers
- three different-sized teddy bears.

What you do

- Read the story of *Goldilocks and the Three Bears*. Explain that you are going to work together to construct chairs for the different-sized bears that you have.

- Show the children how to make a simple framework with the garden wire and use rolled, folded, woven and plaited newspaper to make a chair strong enough to hold each bear.

- Place each bear in his chair. Does he fit? Do you need to make the chair stronger by adding more wire or paper?

And another idea

Use the different-sized chairs when you act out the story of *Goldilocks* (see Drama and role-play, The three bears' cottage, page 48).

Mr Bear, are you there?

ELG: CD 1, 2, 4

What you need
- blindfold.

What you do

Sit in a circle with the children and sing this song together, to the tune of 'Tommy Thumb':

> Mr Bear, Mr Bear,
> Are you there?
> Here I am, here I am.
> Who goes there?

Invite a volunteer to sit in the middle of the circle and be Mr Bear. They must pretend to be asleep, hibernating in the cave. Ask them to close or cover their eyes. Alternatively use a blindfold.

Point at a child around the circle who has to sing the first two lines of the song on their own.

Mr Bear has to sing the next two lines and then guess who was singing to him. Can he identify the soloist correctly? If he can, they have to take a turn at being Mr Bear.

And another idea
Place a small pot behind the sleeping bear. Can a child creep up and steal it without him waking up. This can be made harder by filling the pot with bells that jingle when the pot is moved.

Dancing bears
ELG: CD 1, 2, 3

What you need
- copy of 'Dancing Bears' by William Holbrook Beard (American artist 1824–1900) available on the Internet at www.artsender.com
- CD of classical 'Bear' music (see PD, Dancing with bears, page 31)
- paper
- paints.

What you do

- Talk about the picture of the dancing bears with the children. Do they think bears really like to dance? Which bears are dancing in the painting? What are the other bears doing? Do the children think polar bears dance on the ice?

- Listen to some of the classical music inspired by bears. It certainly sounds like they are dancing. Talk about the strong beat and rhythm in the music and the changes in tempo.

- Play the music as the children paint some pictures of dancing bears. How can they make their bears look as though they are dancing?

And another idea
Find some other paintings or artwork inspired by bears to stimulate the children's creative development.

Bears' portrait gallery

ELG: CD 1, 2, 3

What you need
- lots of teddy bears
- easels
- paints
- pastels
- pens
- large sheets of paper
- gold or silver card
- pasta
- gold spray paint.

What you do

- Using easels and large pieces of paper invite the children to draw or paint a portrait of their special bear.

- Look at famous portraits of people by artists such as Matisse, Picasso, Da Vinci, Warhol and Van Gogh.

- Let the children choose bold colours and different styles to paint portraits of their bears. Can they use their pencil or paints to create furry and fluffy textures?

- Invite some of the children to paint pictures of each other holding their bears.

- Help the children to construct picture frames using gold or silver card, or plain card with pasta glued on and sprayed with gold paint.

- Display the portraits on the wall like an art gallery. Invite parents and carers to visit your setting and admire the children's work.

And another idea
Design a brochure for the portrait gallery listing all the children's work.

Bear prints

ELG: CD 1, 2, 3

What you need

- photocopiable bear template (see page 79)
- cardboard
- scissors
- brown, black or white finger paint
- shiny paper
- combs
- forks
- paper.

What you do

- Use the bear template from page 79 to cut out different-sized bears from thick cardboard.

- Spread thick brown, black or white finger paint on a flat surface of shiny paper or a washable table.

- Invite the children to make patterns like a bear's fur in the paint using fingers and a variety of tools such as combs, forks, and home made card combs.

- Press the bear shapes on to the swirly paint and then print the bears on to paper.

And another idea

Mount the bears on the wall and create a bear display. Learn the poem 'Bears on parade' (see Stories, songs and rhymes page 72) and add the words to the display.

 38 Creative Development

Beat bears

ELG: CD 4

What you need

- a set of beanbag bears, either home-made or use beanie baby bears!

What you do

- If you can't find any bear shaped beanbags, try drawing bear faces on ordinary bean bags. The important thing is the children need weighted bags to help feel the beat as they try these musical games.

- Ask the children to tap the beat on their hands or knees in time to a simple song or rhyme. Try the following to the tune of 'It's raining, it's pouring':

  Beat bears, beat bears,

  Can you keep the beat bears?

  Keep it with your hands bears,

  1, 2, 3, 4

  Change the part of the body in the rhyme each time.

- Try this with any favourite songs and rhymes about bears.

And another idea

Ask the children to march around in a circle in time to a drumbeat. Can they take their beat bears with them and tap them in time as they go? What happens when you change the tempo?

Bear art

ELG: CD 1, 2, 3

What you need
- pictures or examples of Native American art inspired by bears (www.freespiritgallery.ca/nativeamericanbear.htm)
- photocopiable bear templates (see pages 77, 79 and 80)
- cotton wool buds
- paints in primary colours
- black sugar paper.

What you do

- Explain that the bear is a central figure of many Native American Indian rituals and is a symbol of power, strength, modesty (not boasting) and healing.

- The image of the bear has inspired lots of artwork on totem poles, plaques, drawings, masks, jewellery, art and carvings. Look at examples in books and online.

- Help the children to use the bear templates on pages 77, 79 and 80 to cut out a bear shape in black sugar paper. They can get creative with the cotton wool buds to make spots, stripes and simple small shapes on their bear using very bold primary colours.

And another idea
Construct a totem pole using large empty tins and stick the painted bears on to the structure.

Bear trails

ELGs: CD 2, 3; PD 2, 4

What you need

- large potatoes
- paper
- paints
- laminator
- treasure!

What you do

- Prepare the potato prints for the children by cutting the potatoes in half and carving the shapes of bear paw prints into them (see diagram). Dip the potatoes into the paint and print the paws on to paper or card. Help the children to cut them out.

- Alternatively, use thumb and fingerprints and thick brown paint to create paw print shapes.

- Laminate the best paw prints.

- Go outside and lay a trail of bear prints around the area for children to follow. Ask them to create new trails for each other. Will the trails go up, down, over and through equipment?

- Talk about where the bears might be going and what they might see. Add simple written or picture clues along the way for the children to follow.

- Leave treasure at the end for the children to find.

And another idea

Use playground chalk to draw paths for the children to follow through the outside area. Ask the children to add chalk trees, plants, signs and landmarks for each other to follow. Can they draw a map or write instructions?

Parachute games

ELGs: PD 2, 4, 7; CD 4

What you need
- small parachute or sari cut in half and sewn into a square
- lots of small teddy bears

What you do

- Sit in a circle and ask each child to hold the edge of the parachute or sari. Practise moving or floating the fabric up and down together.

- Place one bear in the middle and try making it jump up and down as you sing this song to the tune of 'Skip to my lou'.

- 'One little bear, jumping up and down', (repeat three times) 'Calls for another bear to play'.

- Then add another bear and change the words to 'Two little bears' and so on.

- Try bouncing all the bears together and sing 'Lots of bears'!

And another idea
Slow it right down and gently rock the fabric from side to side as you sing
'All the bears have gone to sleep' (repeat three times)
'Now it's time to wake them up!'
Finish by vigorously waking the bears up again!

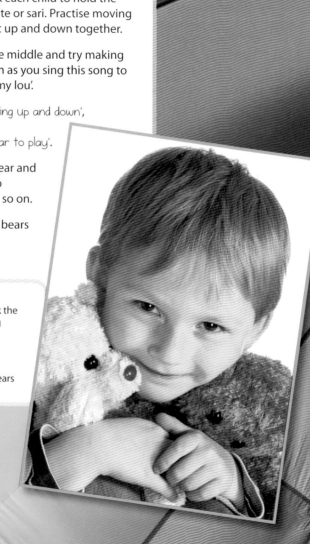

Ready teddy go

ELGs: PSED 2, 8, 11; PD 1, 2, 5, 6

What you need
- teddy bears
- small equipment (balls, bats, hoops, ropes, quoits).

What you do

- Talk to the children about organising some simple races at the Teddy Bear's picnic (see PSED, Teddy bear's picnic, page 9) for them and their bears.

- Ask the children to carry their bears and try running races of different distances. Add obstacles such as hoops and tunnels for them to jump or crawl through.

- Try these Balancing Bears games. Place teddy bears on small quoits and see who can carry their bears to the finishing line without dropping them.

- Stretch out skipping ropes on the ground and ask the children to walk along them carrying their bears. Try again with balance beams.

And another idea
Can the children make up some races and games of their own to try with the bears at the Teddy Bear's picnic?

Hide and seek

ELGs: PSED 8, 12; PSRN 12; CD 4

What you need
- teddy bear
- outside area.

What you do

- Choose a bear to play hide and seek.

- Start off by hiding the bear outside in a variety of places – under bushes, behind trees, in front of pots, on play equipment, in holes, beside flowers, inside buckets and so on.

- Ask the children to work with a partner to try to find the bear and then describe where they found him using positional language.

- Take it in turns to hide the bear again for others to find.

- Try singing this song to the tune of 'Frere Jacques'

  Where is teddy? Where is teddy?
  He's not here! He's not here!
  Where is teddy hiding? Where is teddy hiding?
  It's not clear! It's not clear!

- Ask for a volunteer to hide the bear and then give the group verbal or written clues to help them find it.

And another idea
Ask the children to find a good hiding place outside for both themselves and the bear. Remind them of where they are allowed to go in the outside area to keep safe.

Shadow bears

ELGs: KUW 1, 2, 3, 4; CD 1, 3; PD 1, 4

What you need

- teddy bears
- chalk
- water
- paintbrushes.

What you do

- Choose a sunny day and go outside on to the playground or similar outdoor area. Make sure each child has a teddy bear.

- Look at the shadows created by the sun shining on the children and then compare this with the shadows cast by the teddy bears.

- Invite the children to draw round the teddy bears' shadows using chalk or paint them with water. Which bear casts the biggest or funniest shape shadow?

- What happens when the sun goes behind a cloud? How long do the paintings stay on the ground?

And another idea

Play 'shadow tag'. Ask for a volunteer to be 'it' and tell them to try and jump on as many shadows as they can. If your shadow is jumped on you have to sit out and cheer everyone else on!

Outdoor art

ELGs: PSED 8; CD 1, 2, 3

What you need

- lots of natural materials
- plastic sheet
- string
- wire
- glue.

What you do

- Look at examples of work by famous artists such as Andy Goldsworthy and Helen Denerley who use found materials in their sculptures. Go to www.funksculp.com to look at animals and figures sculpted from junk metal.

- Go outside and collect together lots of different natural materials such as stones, twigs, leaves, grass, nuts, acorns, flowers, moss, feathers and so on.

- In small groups lay out all your materials on a plastic sheet and try to form them into the shape of a bear. Find ways to join materials together using string, wire, glue and so on.

- Photograph the bear pictures or sculptures.

And another idea

Provide children with plastic gloves so that they can safely pick up litter and use these items in a junk or recycled picture of a bear.

Bear cave

ELGs: PSED 4; CLL 4, 7; KUW 2, 9; CD 5

What you need

- dark drapes, curtains, screens and climbing frame to create cave space
- cushions
- luminous stars
- torches
- teddy bears
- storybooks including *When Will It Be Spring?* by Catherine Walters (Dutton Juvenile).

What you do

- Create a dark, cosy bear's cave in a quiet corner filled with cushions, torches, bears and storybooks.

- Introduce the bear cave to the children and talk about how some bears hibernate over the cold winter months. Explain that baby bears are usually born during hibernation in the cave and then emerge in the spring.

- Encourage children to use these facts in their role-play in the cave. How do they think baby bear will feel when he comes out of the cave for the first time? Can they describe how it feels to live in a cave?

- Talk about light and dark. Try performing different actions in the light and then in the dark, by closing their eyes or wearing a blindfold. The children could try putting on a jumper/coat, writing their name or having a drink!

- Read *When Will It Be Spring?* by Catherine Walters (Dutton Juvenile) and act out the adventures of Alfie as he impatiently waits for spring to come.

And another idea

Read *Can't you sleep, Little Bear?* or *Sleep tight, Little Bear* both by Martin Waddell (Walker Books). Talk about feeling scared of the dark or being on your own and encourage children to share their feelings through drama. Act out the stories in the Bear cave.

The three bears' cottage

ELGs: PSED 9; CLL 4, 7, 8; CD 5

What you need

- story of *Goldilocks and the Three Bears*
- three different-sized bowls, chairs, beds and teddy bears
- brown fun fur tabards
- furry gloves
- slippers, curly yellow wig and dress for Goldilocks
- other home corner furniture
- brown fun fur, wool, and felt
- scissors
- paper plates and card
- paint
- stapler
- elastic.

What you do

- Tell or read the story of *Goldilocks and the Three Bears* to the children and then let them help you set up the home corner as the bear's cottage.

- Make bear masks by cutting bear faces out of card or using paper plates. Encourage the children to decorate these with brown materials such as fun fur, wool, felt and paint. Staple on ears and fasten with elastic.

- Invite the children to act out the story in the cottage. Encourage them to use different voices for the three bears.

- Talk about the feelings of the different characters. Go into role as a newspaper reporter (dress up in a coat and use a microphone) and interview the bears and Goldilocks. How did baby bear feel when he saw his broken chair? Is Goldilocks sorry for what she did?

And another idea

Ask children to have a go at interviewing each other as different characters. Extend this to other traditional stories. Who would they like to interview?

Goldilocks and the Three Bears

Teddy bear factory and shop

ELGs: CLL 7, 18; PSRN 2, 3, 4; CD 4, 5; PD 2

What you need

- lots of different-sized teddy bears
- shelving/plastic bins
- labels
- money
- till
- materials and play equipment to build machines.

What you do

● Introduce the idea of a factory where teddy bears are made. What sort of things would they expect to see in the factory?

● Ask the children to work with a partner and invent a machine movement and sound. Combine all the pairs into a giant moving teddy bear machine. Practise stopping and starting the machine.

● Build a machine for the factory using play equipment. Construct a conveyor belt using a slide and position the teddy bears along it. Make up suitable sound effects.

● Display the teddy bears in the factory shop on shelves or in plastic bins. Make price labels. Talk about different roles children can play in the factory and shop. Try introducing fussy customers and grumpy shop assistants.

And another idea

Sing this song to the tune of 'How Much Is That Doggy in the Window':

How much is that teddy in the window?

The one with the beautiful bow.

How much is that teddy in the window?

I really, I really must know.

Bears' hospital

ELGs: PSED 5, 11; CLL 5, 6, 7, 18; CD 5

What you need
- different-sized teddy bears
- beds
- cots
- bedding
- bandages
- doctor's equipment cases
- dressing-up clothes.

What you do

- Work with the children to set up a hospital ward for all the teddy bears. Use dolls' beds and cots. Add doctors' white coats and equipment and nurses' uniforms for the children to dress up in.

- Make up different illnesses and help the children to write a chart for each bear including its name and simple details of treatment attached to a clipboard. These can be left by each poorly bear's bed.

- Invite the children to take on the roles of doctors, nurses and visitors.

- Try some improvised drama stories in the hospital involving an angry patient, a chatty nurse, a lost visitor, a grateful patient or a rude doctor.

And another idea
Try singing and acting out the song 'Ten bears in the bed' (see Stories, songs and rhymes, page 70) using children or bears!

Guess the tale

ELGs: PSED 8; CLL 3, 4, 7, 13; CD 5

What you need
- lots of different props related to storybooks.

What you do

- Explain to the children that you are going to play a guessing game involving lots of different stories about bears. Recap a few of them before you start.

- Sit in a circle and put props from a story in the middle for them to look at such as a bowl and spoon, chair, golden wig, box of porridge. Who can guess the tale?

- Invite the child to choose a prop and then ask them to 'go into character' and say an appropriate line or tell part of the story. Can the other children guess who they are pretending to be?

- Try again with other sets of props, for example, owl, cardboard box, boots, colander (*Whatever Next!* by Jill Murphy) or lantern, pillow, storybook (*Can't you sleep, Little Bear?* by Martin Waddell) or teddy bear, chair, owl, trombone (*This Is The Bear and The Scary Night* by Sarah Hayes).

And another idea
Play 'guess the prop'. Put the props in a feely bag or box and invite the children to put in their hand, feel an item and try to describe it for the others to guess, without actually saying its name.

Polar bears

ELGs: PSED 4; KUW 6, 9, 10; CD 2, 5

What you need
- Copy of *The Polar Bear and the Snow Cloud* by Jane Cabrera (Macmillan)
- large sheet of white paper
- scissors
- small white sheet.

What you do

- Read the story of *The Polar Bear and the Snow Cloud*. This is the story of a lonely polar bear cub. The snow cloud tries to help him find a friend by making animal shapes out of snow.

- Talk about feeling lonely with the children and how we all need friends. How do they think it would feel to live all alone in the Arctic?

- Act out the story of the lonely polar bear in the snow. Take turns to cut out shapes from the white paper to make snow friends for the polar bear.

- Alternatively, place a white sheet over one or more children and ask them to use their bodies to make the shape of the different friends!

And another idea
Choose another book about polar bears (see Useful books, page 75) and try some physical drama. Try sliding on the 'ice' using metal trays or a large sheet of aluminium foil. Hold child's feet and let them slide down the 'ice' on their bottom!

Gingerbread bears

ELGs: PSED 8; PSRN 1; KUW 3; CD 5

What you need

- baking tray
- parchment
- bear-shaped cutters
- 125g unsalted butter
- 100g dark brown sugar
- 4tbsp golden syrup
- 325g plain flour
- 1tsp bicarbonate of soda
- 2tsp ground ginger.

Make sure children are supervised at all times when involved in cooking activities. Always be extra careful with tools, electrical equipment and all sources of heat! Remind them to wash their hands before starting to handle any food or equipment. Check for food allergies before doing the activities and tasting any food.

What you do

- Pre-heat oven 170°C/Gas mark 3 and line the baking tray with parchment.

- Melt the butter, sugar and syrup in a saucepan and then remove from the heat.

- Sieve the dry ingredients into a bowl and stir in the melted butter mixture carefully to make a stiff dough.

- Turn out on to a floured surface and roll out to a thickness of roughly 5mm.

- Cut out bear shapes using the cutter and place the biscuits on the baking tray.

- Bake for 10 minutes until light golden brown.

And another idea

Use icing and decorations to decorate with bear faces, fur, clothes, and so on. Chocolate hundreds and thousands make good furry bears!

Porridge flapjack

ELGs: PSED 8; PSRN 6; KUW 3.

What you need
- shallow baking tin
- 125g butter or margarine
- 60g Demerara sugar
- 1tbsp golden syrup
- 250g porridge oats
- 90g raisins
- 1tsp salt.

What you do

- Pre-heat oven 180°C/Gas mark 4 and grease a shallow baking tin.

- Gently melt the butter, sugar and syrup together in a large saucepan over a low heat.

- Remove from the heat and carefully stir in the oats, raisins and salt until combined.

- Pour into the tin and press down.

- Bake for 20 minutes. Cut into squares and leave to cool.

And another idea
Try making some porridge. Mix together one cup of oats, with one cup of milk and one cup of water. Heat gently and stir until mixture thickens. Serve with toppings of sugar, honey, syrup, jam or salt. Which topping do the children like best?

Honey scones

ELGs: PSED 8; CLL 1; PSRN 1; KUW 3; PD 8

What you need

- baking tray
- cutter
- 250g self raising flour
- 1/2tsp salt
- 30g butter or margarine
- 1tbsp castor sugar
- 2tbsp raisins
- 1tbsp runny honey
- 1 egg
- 4tbsp milk.

What you do

- Pre-heat the oven to 200°C/ Gas mark 6 and grease the baking tray.

- Sift the flour and salt into a mixing bowl.

- Rub the butter into the dry mixture and add the sugar and raisins.

- Mix well and make a well in the middle.

- Whisk together the honey, egg and enough milk to make 150ml of liquid.

- Pour the liquid into the well in the flour and mix into a dough using a fork. Knead on a floured surface into a smooth dough.

- Lightly roll out the dough to a thickness of 1 to 2cm and cut out 10 to 12 scones using the cutters.

- Dust the scones with flour and bake for 12 minutes.

- Serve warm, cut in half, with butter and more honey!

And another idea

Choose some other flavours for your scones such as cheese or marmite.

Pizza bears

ELGs: PSED 12; KUW 6; PD 8; CD 2

What you need

- bear-shaped cutter or photocopiable bear template (see page 79)
- scissors
- wholemeal pitta breads
- tomato puree or jar of ragout
- grated cheese
- other pizza toppings, such as cubes of ham, bacon, slices of pepperoni, sweetcorn or pineapple.

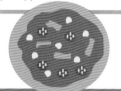

What you do

- Use the cutter to cut out bear shapes from the pitta bread. Alternatively, draw around the cutter or bear template on to the bread using edible pens and help the children to cut around the shape.

- Spread tomato sauce on to the bread and sprinkle on grated cheese.

- Add other pizza toppings such as cubes of ham, bacon, slices of pepperoni, sweetcorn or pineapple.

- Grill for two minutes until the cheese has melted.

And another idea

Just make the bear face using the same pizza ingredients but on a round base such as a crumpet or half a muffin. What could you use to make the bear's ears?

Big Ted's Pizza Recipes

Frozen bears

ELGs: PSRN 4, 11; KUW 1, 2, 3, 4

What you need

- plastic polar bears
- clear plastic take-away food trays
- water tray
- deep freezer
- ice cube trays
- white powder paint.

What you do

- Place each polar bear in a plastic take-away food tray filled with cold water and freeze until solid.

- Put the frozen bear blocks into the water tray and watch them melt gradually. Time how long it takes for each ice block to melt or thaw. Talk about the changes the children can see as they play.

- Make icebergs using different-sized and shaped ice cube trays filled with white powder paint mixed with cold water and then frozen.

- Float the homemade icebergs on the water to create a realistic Arctic environment for the polar bears to climb on.

And another idea

Investigate what happens if you add warm or hot water to the water tray. What do the children think will happen? Alternatively, line a tuff spot with aluminium foil and sprinkle with cornflour. Pile up several blocks of ice into an ice mountain for the polar bears to climb on.

Porridge play

What you need
- shallow tray
- porridge oats
- different-sized spoons
- bowls
- jugs
- pots
- plastic bottles
- three different-sized teddy bears.

What you do

- Fill a shallow tray on a table top with dry porridge oats and lots of different containers and implements.

- Invite the children to make some porridge for the three bears. Who will have the biggest bowl?

- Ask them to experiment with the different materials and containers.

- Can they count how many spoons it takes to fill each bowl, pot or jug?

- Can they give each other instructions to follow such as 'put four big spoons of oats into this jug and then add two more' and so on.

- At the end of the session provide some small bottles of water and let the children observe the changes when they add water to the dry oats.

And another idea
Make some porridge with the children (see Cooking, Porridge flapjack, page 54). Repeat this activity with other messy materials such as dry or cooked pasta, tinned rice pudding, baked beans or spaghetti, dried beans and lentils.

Bear habitats

ELGs: KUW 2, 9; PD 7, 8

What you need

- sand tray
- wet sand
- small-world plastic bears
- white plastic trays
- spades
- plastic pots
- twigs.

What you do

- Talk to the children about the different habitats that bears live in (see KUW, Bears around the world, page 25).

- Ask them to try to build a cave and some holes in the wet sand tray for the plastic bears to hibernate in.

- Show them how to use pots on their side covered with sand for caves. How will they make a door for the cave?

- Can they use twigs for trees and balance the bears on them?

And another idea

Bury some bears in the sand and then use another bear to make tracks of paw prints for the children to follow to find the hidden bears.

Muddy prints

ELGs: PSED 11; PD 1, 2; CD 1, 2

What you need
- shallow tray or tuff spot
- clean soil or compost
- roll of lining paper
- bowls of warm soapy water
- towels.

What you do

● Fill your shallow tray or tuff spot with soil or compost for the children to handle, explore and dig.

● Explain to the children that you are going to make some muddy paw prints. Ask them to remove their shoes and socks and roll up any long sleeves.

● Add a small amount of water and let the children put their bare hands and feet into the mud and then walk along the roll of lining paper on all fours like bears to create hand and foot prints.

● At the end of the roll of paper prepare a cleaning area with another tray full of warm soapy water and some towels so the children can wash off the mud!

And another idea
Make block prints using thick card, string and glue. Stick the string on to a small square of card in a spiral shape for the main pad of the paw and then five strips of string or elastic band for the claws. Press into the mud mixture and then print on to sheets of white paper.

Inuit bear sculptures

ELGs: PD 8; CD 1, 2, 3

What you need
- pictures or images of Inuit bear art
- white play dough.

What you do

○ Show children images of Inuit art at www. inuitartsculptures.com and look at the polar bear sculptures. Talk about the Inuit people who inhabit the frozen north of Canada and the Arctic where the polar bears live.

○ Make some very white play dough using cornflour instead of normal flour and encourage the children to make their own bear sculptures!

And another idea
Make some salt flour dough using cornflour. Mix together one cup of plain flour, one cup of cornflour, one cup of salt and then gradually add one cup of cold water. Knead into a soft dough. Alternatively, use normal salt flour dough or clay and paint the finished artworks with white paint.

How the Bear Lost His Tail

Native American legend retold by Judith Harries

A long time ago Bear had a beautiful long bushy tail, which he was very proud of. He would show it off to everybody and boast 'Don't you think this is the most beautiful tail you've ever seen?'

The other animals were too scared of Bear and his sharp claws so they all agreed. All except Fox who decided to play a trick on Bear.

It was winter time and the spirit of the frost had swept across the land and covered everywhere with thick ice. Fox made a hole in the ice and when Bear came lumbering up to the lake he saw him surrounded by lots of fish, juicy trout and fat perch. Just then Fox pulled his tail out of the hole and landed yet another huge fish in front of Bear.

'Greetings Brother Fox,' said Bear, with his mouth watering. 'What are you doing?'

'I am fishing,' said Fox. 'Would you like to have a go?'

'But you don't have anything to fish with,' said Bear.

'I used my tail,' said Fox. 'Shall I show you?'

Bear moved hungrily towards the hole in the ice.

'Wait,' said Fox. 'There's no fish left here. Let's find a new fishing spot for you.'

Fox led Bear to a place where he knew the water was too shallow for winter fish and dug a new hole.

'Now sit here with your back to the hole and put your tail in the water. Try not to think about fish as they can read your thoughts. Be patient.'

Fox went and sat behind the bushes and watched Bear sitting still with his beautiful tail in the hole and Fox laughed and laughed. Soon Fox got tired and went home.

Bear too felt tired and went to sleep. The night grew colder and colder. In the morning Fox returned to see if Bear was still there. There was a mound of snow on the lake under which Bear still sat waiting to catch his fill of fish.

Fox crept up behind Bear and shouted 'Bear! Bear! I can see the fish! Pull your tail up now!'

Hearing Fox's shouts, Bear woke up and tried to pull his tail out of the water. But his tail had been caught in the ice, which had frozen over in the night, and all Bear heard was a sharp 'snap' as his tail broke off!

'Oh no! My beautiful tail! Fox, I will get you for this!'

But Fox was too quick and off he ran. So it is to this day that Bear has no tail and is definitely not a friend of Fox!

Baby Bear is Best

A new story by Mel Astill

Baby Bear really disliked his name. He was given to Luka on the day he was born by his Grandma. Small and blue with a ribbon tied round his neck, he had been Luka's favourite bear for cuddling, sleeping next to, rolling on to, chewing and throwing out of his cot.

'Baby! What a silly name for a bear! What a silly name to call me!' Baby Bear thought.

Luka was three now and Grandma (and Grandad!) had given him quite a few more bears.

'Far too many,' thought Baby Bear, 'And their names are all far more exciting than mine!'

There was Brandon, a big, strong-looking brown bear; Arnold, with legs that moved and a head that turned; Bobby, who growled when his tummy was pressed. And now Luka had another brand new bear, Bonnie, who actually sang songs when her paws were held!

'Luka will never play with me or cuddle me again, not now he has all these exciting bears,' thought Baby sadly. He sat on the end of Luka's bed waiting to be chosen for a game or a cuddle… but Luka seemed to have forgotten his small, blue Baby Bear.

He chose Brandon bear to play when his friend Theo came round. He chose Arnold to take out to the park for an adventure. Luka wanted Bobby to sit at the table with him for lunch and he chose Bonnie for just about everything else. Baby bear was very sad and very lonely.

One morning Luka didn't choose any of his bears and it was very quiet in the house. Baby Bear looked up as Luka's Mummy came into the bedroom; she seemed to be looking for something. All of a sudden Baby Bear found himself being lifted up and taken to the top of the bed.

'Ah! There you are Baby, Luka has been asking for you. He has been feeling poorly and is waiting for a cuddle.' Mummy placed Baby Bear next to Luka, who reached out and gave him the biggest cuddle ever!

'Baby Bear is best for cuddles!' said Luka happily.

'Baby Bear likes cuddles best!' thought Baby Bear.

Polar Bear's Journey

A new story by Judith Harries

Nils, the baby polar bear, lay back in his blanket of snow and waited. He was waiting for his mother. He was very still and quiet, almost as if frozen. The only things moving were his ears twitching as they strained to hear every sound coming from the icy wastes around him. Mother had said she would return very soon but it seemed like hours had passed and there was still no sign of her. Now he was worried.

'Crack!' Nils opened one eye and listened carefully.

'Crack! Creak!' Nils opened his other eye and sat up. He saw a crack in the ice next to him and watched as it grew bigger.

'Crack! Creak! Clunk!' The crack grew bigger until eventually the piece of ice he was sitting on broke off. Nils found himself on an island, drifting away.

'Mother,' he shouted. 'Where are you?' He listened and heard his own voice echo back 'Mother! Where are you?'

And then there was silence... until Nils heard a voice from behind him.

'Hey baby bear, you're looking blue. Where are you off to?' said the large hairy walrus sitting on the ice.

'I'm looking for my mother. Have you seen her?'

'I have indeed. Why don't you follow me?'

So Nils used his paws and began to row the ice island after the walrus, off to find his mother. Then he heard more voices behind him and stopped.

'Hey baby bear, you're looking blue. Where are you and walrus off to?' said the two arctic hares, their long white ears standing up tall.

'I'm looking for my mother. Walrus has seen her!'

'Can we come and help?' asked the hares.

So Nils invited the hares on to his island and they all began to row after the walrus, off to find his mother. Then he heard more voices behind him and stopped.

'Hey baby bear, you're looking blue. Where are you and walrus and the hares off to?' said three arctic foxes, swishing their fluffy white tails to and fro in the snow.

'I'm looking for my mother. Walrus has seen her!'

'Can we come and help?' asked the foxes.

So Nils invited the foxes on to his island and they all began to row after the walrus, off to find his mother. The island was getting rather crowded. Then he heard more voices behind him and stopped.

'Hey baby bear, you're looking blue. Where are you and walrus and the hares and the foxes all off to?' said four lemmings, their whiskers twitching with excitement.

'I'm looking for my mother. Walrus has seen her!'

'Can we come and follow?' asked the lemmings.

So Nils invited the lemmings on to his island and they all began to row after the walrus, off to find his mother. But now the island was so packed with animals that it began to rock and sway and wobble this way and that until, with an almighty splash, all the animals fell into the water.

Nils felt something big and soft and furry all around him, and it lifted him out of the water and plonked him down safely on the ice. It was Mother, looking so pleased to see him.

'Oh Nils, I was looking for you everywhere. I am so glad you're safe. Where were you and walrus and the hares and the foxes and the lemmings all off to?' Mother asked. As she spoke, all the animals clambered out of the water with the help of the walrus and gathered around Nils and his mother.

'We were looking for you!' they all cried.

Masha and the Bear

Traditional Russian fairy tale retold by Judith Harries

Once upon a time there was a little girl called Masha who lived with her grandparents in a village near a big, dark forest. One day she went into the forest with her friends to gather berries and mushrooms. As she searched from bush to bush and tree to tree she wandered further into the forest and away from all the other children. She called out their names but they did not reply. She was completely lost!

She walked on into the heart of the forest and found a little wooden house. She knocked on the door, but there was no reply. She opened the door, went inside and sat down on a bench by the window.

That evening the great big bear who the house belonged to returned home and was delighted to see little Masha.

'Aha,' he said, 'now you must stay here and work for me, cleaning the house and making my porridge every day!'

Little Masha wept but she had no choice and had to stay. Each day the bear went out into the forest and told Masha not to leave the house.

'If you go out, I will soon find you and eat you!'

Little Masha thought hard and came up with a clever plan!

She asked the bear if she could go back to her village and take her grandparents some of her tasty home baked pies.

'No, no!' said the bear, 'you might lose your way. I will take the pies to them myself'. Masha smiled. That was the first part of her clever plan.

So she baked the pies and chose a big basket to put them in for the bear to carry on his back.

'I shall put the pies in this basket. Make sure you don't eat any of them on the way. I shall climb to the top of that tall tree and watch you all the way!'

'Alright,' said the bear. 'Give me the basket.'

'Just go outside and check if it's raining.'

While the bear was outside, Masha jumped into the basket and pulled the pies on top of her. The bear returned, picked up the basket and set off. He wandered past all the fir trees – tramp, tramp, tramp. He wandered past the birch trees – clomp, clomp, clomp. He clambered up and down hill, and began to tire.

'I'm so tired, I must rest, I'll eat a pie, that'd be best!'

But Masha shouted out from inside the basket.

'I can see you from way up high.

Don't you dare eat a pie!'

'What amazing eyesight she must have!' thought the bear. 'She can see everything!' He lifted up the basket and set off again. He wandered past more trees – tramp, tramp, tramp, clomp, clomp, clomp. Then he felt very tired.

'I'm so tired, I must rest, I'll eat a pie, that'd be best!'

But Masha shouted out from inside the basket.

'I can see you from way up high.

Don't you dare eat a pie!'

The bear was astonished. She must have climbed up very high to see this far away. He reached the village and found Masha's house. He knocked on the gate very hard and called out 'Hello, I've brought you a gift from little Masha.'

The dogs in the village smelt the bear and rushed up to the house from every direction barking and barking. The bear put down the basket and ran back to the forest as fast as he could. Masha's grandparents came out of their house and found the basket by the gate.

'What's in here?' asked the old woman. She looked in the basket and saw the pies and then could not believe her eyes. There sat Masha in the basket, safe and well and full of smiles!

Winter's Here

(Tune: Frère Jacques)

Are you sleeping? *(repeat twice)*
Mother bear *(repeat twice)*
Weather's getting colder *(repeat twice)*
Winter's here. *(repeat twice)*

In the dark cave, *(repeat twice)*
Mother bear *(repeat twice)*
Sleep in here 'til Springtime *(repeat twice)*
Winter's here. *(repeat twice)*

Time to wake now, *(repeat twice)*
Mother bear *(repeat twice)*
Wake up all your cubs now *(repeat twice)*
Spring is here. *(repeat twice)*

Ten Bears in the Bed

(Tune: Ten in the bed)

Ten bears in the bed
And the little one said.
'Roll over, roll over!'
So they all rolled over
And one fell out….

Naming Song

(Tune: Do You Know the Muffin Man?)

Can you name this teddy bear,
This teddy bear, this teddy bear?
Can you name this teddy bear,
Let us call him……………..

Bears Around the World

(Tune: Tommy Thumb)

Polar bear, are you there?
In the snow.
Sliding here, sliding there,
Nice and slow.

Black bear, are you there?
Up the tree,
Climbing high, climbing low,
I can see.

Grizzly bear, are you there?
Growling loud,
Catching salmon, shiny fish,
Standing proud.

Panda bear, are you there?
Eating bamboo,
Munching leaves, crunching shoots,
Where are you?

B.E.A.R.S

(Tune: B.I.N.G.O)

My favourite toys, I have to say,
Are definitely bears.
B.E.A.R.S., B.E.A.R.S., B.E.A.R.S.,
Teddy bears are best!

Bears on Parade

(Tune: Aiken Drum)

Marching here and marching there,
Marching nearly everywhere,
Marching in and out the square,
The bears are on parade.

Marching up and marching down,
Marching all about the town,
Marching there and all around,
The bears are on parade.

Marching high and marching low,
Marching fast and marching slow,
Marching everywhere they go,
The bears are on parade.

Action Bears

Big bears, small bears, furry bears… prowl
Brown bears, grizzly bears, polar bears… growl
Marching bears, jumping bears, skipping bears… hop
Slow bears, fast bears, bouncing bears… STOP!
Quiet bears, lazy bears, yawning bears… creep
Cuddly bears, snuggly bears, tired bears… sleep.
Mel Astill

Balancing Bears

Bear on a tightrope
Bear in a tree
Bear in a dark cave
Can't catch me!

Bear on an iceberg
Bear up a hill
Bear goes fishing
Catch me if you will!

Best Bears

My best bear,
Sits on a chair,
And waits for me all day.
My special ted,
Lies on the bed,
He never goes away.

My best bear
Is always there.
He cheers me when I'm sad.
My special ted,
It must be said,
Makes me feel so glad.

ICT resources and ideas

Meet Paddington Bear

ELGs: CLL 3, 4; KUW 7; PD 2

Website:
www.paddingtonbear.com

- Visit this official website for Paddington Bear. Go to Make and Do and try out some of the activities.

- Play a game of pairs – 'Matching Bears'.

- Improve your 'mouse' control by playing 'Marmalade Mayhem'.

Bear information

ELGs: KUW 7, 9

Website: www.bears.org

- Useful information about different species of bears around the world including facts and pictures.

Website:
www.bearplanet.org

- More pictures and facts about different bears and useful connections to other helpful sites.

Website:
www.kidzone.ws/lw/bears

- Look at Bear Facts and Bear Photos for a great collection of information and photographs.

Winnie the Pooh

ELGs: CLL 4, 8; KUW 7

Website: www.pooh75.com

- Visit this special site to celebrate 75 years of Winnie the Pooh using the original E H Shepard illustrations.

- Try some of the online games and listen to the stories.

Bear puzzles

ELGs: KUW 7, 9; PD2

Website:
www.dltk-kids.com/
puzzles/polar-cubs.htm

- Try the online jigsaw puzzle of a polar bear and cubs. Change the number of pieces and types of cut to vary the difficulty.

History of the teddy bear

ELGs: KUW 7, 8, 9; CD 2, 3

Website:
www.theodoreroosevelt.org

- Follow links - Just for Kids - Real story of teddy bear.

- Research the story of the origins of the teddy bear and look at the original cartoon of the American president refusing to shoot a bear while out hunting.

Goldilocks

ELGs: CLL 2, 3, 4; KUW 7

Website:
www.britishcouncil.org/kids-stories-goldilocks.htm

- Read or listen to the story online.

- Print out the activity sheet, look at the pictures from the story and choose the correct captions.

Bears in danger

ELGs: PSED 4, 5, 6; KUW 7, 9, 10

Website: www.wwf.org.uk

- Search for bears and find out which bears are endangered in the world and why.

Bear worksheets

ELGs: CLL 5, 17; KUW 2, 7, 9

Website:
www.kidzone.ws/lw/bears

- Go to Bear activities and look at the different Bear worksheets.

- Print out and make your own Itsy Bitsy Bear Book all about the variety of food that different bears like to eat.

Useful books

Fiction

Paddington Bear (series) by Michael Bond (HarperCollins)

Winnie the Pooh (series) by A A Milne (Egmont Books)

Rupert the Bear (series) (Egmont Books)

Little Polar Bear by Hans de Beer (North-South Books)

Jamberry by Bruce Degen (HarperCollins)

Hamish:The Bear Who Found His Child by Moira Munro (Piccadilly Press Ltd)

Peace at Last by Jill Murphy (Macmillan Children's Books)

Where's My Teddy? (series) by Jez Alborough (Walker Books Ltd)

This Is The Bear (series) by Sarah Hayes (Walker Books Ltd)

Bear by Mick Inkpen (Hodder Children's Books)

One Bear at Bedtime by Mick Inkpen (Hodder Children's Books)

Threadbear by Mick Inkpen (Hodder Children's Books)

Little Bear Lost (series) by Jane Hissey (Red Fox)

Bear Snores On (series) by Karma Wilson (Simon & Schuster)

Big Bear Little Bear by David Bedford (Little Tiger Press)

Mr Bear (series) by Debi Gliori (Orchard)

Can't You Sleep, Little Bear (series) by Martin Waddell (Walker Books Ltd)

I Love My Daddy by Sebastien Braun (Boxer Books Ltd)

The Dancing Bear by Michael Murpurgo (HarperCollins)

Whatever Next! by Jill Murphy (Macmillan Children's Books)

Dear Polar Bear by Barry Ablett (Scholastic)

The Polar Bear Son by Lydia Dabcovich (Houghton Mifflin)

We're Going on a Bear Hunt by Michael Rosen (Walker Books Ltd)

Polar Bear, Polar Bear, What Do You Hear? (series) by Eric Carle (Puffin)

Brown Bear, Brown Bear, What Do You See? by Eric Carle (Puffin)

The Little Mouse, the Red Ripe Strawberry, and the Big Hungry Bear by Audrey Wood (Child's Play)

Useful books (contd.)

Non-fiction

Ice Bear by Nicola Davies (Walker Books Ltd)

The Polar Bear's Home: A Story About Global Warming by Lara Bergen (Little Simon)

The World of the Polar Bear by Norbert Rosing (A & C Black)

Things You Should Know About Bears by Steve Parker (Miles Kelly Publishing Ltd)

Bears of the World by Lance Craighead (Voyageur Press)

Bears: A Year in the Life by Matthias Breiter (A & C Black)

Polar Bears (Our Wild World) by Linda Tagliaferro (Northword)

Bears: Polar Bears, Black Bears and Grizzly Bears by Deborah Hodge (Kids can Press)

Black Bear: North America's Bear by Stephen R Swinburne (Boyds Mills Press)

Giant Pandas by Michelle Levine (Lerner Publications)

Panda (Watch Me Grow) (Dorling Kindersley)

We Are Bears by Molly Grooms (Tormont/ Brimar Publications)

Bear's head

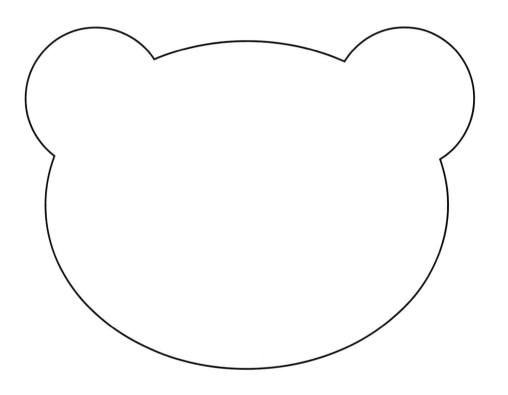

Bear spare parts

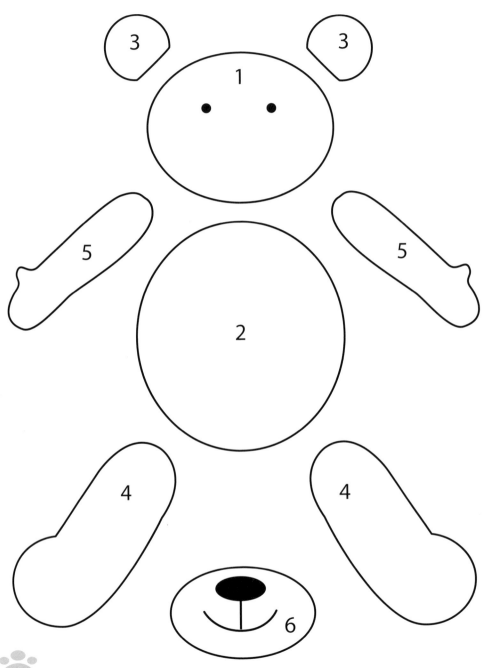

Bear template

Bear profile